30 Lessons
on
Unapologetic Living

LIVING LIFE
WITHOUT
REGRET

EDNA GRAY JAMISON

Published by So It Is Written, LLC
Detroit, MI
SoItIsWritten.net

30 Lessons on Unapologetic Living: Living Life Without Regret
Copyright © 2022 by Edna Gray Jamison

All rights reserved. No part of this book may be reproduced or transmitted in any form or by any means, electronic or mechanical, including photocopying, recording, or by an information storage and retrieval system—except by a reviewer who may quote brief passages in a review to be printed in a magazine or newspaper—without permission in writing from the publisher.

Unless otherwise noted, all Biblical references are quoted from the King James Version.

Edited by: So It Is Written – www.SoItIsWritten.net

Formatting: Ya Ya Ya Creative – www.YaYaYaCreative.com

ISBN: 979-8-9850206-6-3

LCCN: 2022900188

PRINTED AND BOUND IN THE UNITED STATES OF AMERICA

Table of Contents

Introduction 1

Lesson #1: "Unapologetic" 3

Lesson #2: "Unapologetic Praise" 11

Lesson #3: Unapologetic Prayer" 17

Lesson #4: "Unapologetic Hope" 23

Lesson #5: "Unapologetic Love" 29

Lesson #6: "Unapologetic Peace" 35

Lesson #7: "Unapologetic Worship" 41

Lesson #8: "Unapologetic Healing" 47

Lesson #9: "Unapologetic Testimony" 53

Lesson #10: "Unapologetic Change" 59

Lesson #11: "Unapologetic Thanksgiving" 65

Lesson #12: "Unapologetic Provision" 71

Lesson #13: "Unapologetic Favor" 77

Lesson #14: "Unapologetic Protection And Blessings" 83

Lesson #15: "Unapologetic Protection, Blessings And Favor" .. 91

Lesson #16: "Unapologetic Power" 97

Lesson #17: "Unapologetic Witness" 103

Lesson #18: "Unapologetic Prosperity" 109

Lesson #19: "Unapologetically Repentant" 115

Lesson #20: "Unapologetic Love For Others" 121

Lesson #21: "Unapologetic Sanctification" 127

Lesson #22: "Unapologetic Miracles" 133

Lesson #23: "Unapologetic Victory" 139

Lesson #24: "Unapologetic Wisdom" 145

Lesson #25: "Unapologetic Confidence" 151

Lesson #26: "Unapologetic Recovery" 157

Lesson #27: "Unapologetically Silencing The Enemy" 163

Lesson #28: "Unapologetically Inevitable" 169

Lesson #29: "Unapologetic Living" 175

Lesson #30: "Unapologetically His" 181

About The Author 187

Introduction

This series of lessons on "Unapologetic Living" was birthed from an online study called "Graced for Today," which delved into a lifestyle where believers are free to possess what is promised through the Word of God unapologetically.

Each lesson provides thought-provoking, encouraging insights into the posture of the believer. You will be strengthened to ponder deeply into the "land of promise" until you can see yourself taking ownership in every area of life. As you read, digest and ponder each lesson, your desire to dig deeper into the Scriptures will ignite, satiating the part of you that can only be filled with the sweetness and intimacy of God's Word. For truly, "Time spent in the Word of God is never wasted … and you will be 'Graced for Today.'"

LESSON #1
"Unapologetic"

As we begin this lesson, I would like to share my definition of "unapologetic", which will lay the foundation for this study.

Jamison Definition:

Unashamed for your posture, mindset or belief regarding the truth of God's Word; seeing and expecting manifestation because of His favor and faithfulness. Living in a manner and mindset that refuses to apologize for believing to see the goodness of the Lord in the land of the living. Choosing to stand resolute in the face of those who oppose my praise, confidence and my God, yet choosing to humbly love the unloving.

Foundational Scriptures:

Proverbs 5:7-14 (NET)

Key Verses:

¹¹ And at the end of your life you will groan when your flesh and your body are wasted away.

¹⁴ And you will say, "How I hated discipline! My heart spurned reproof!

¹³ For I did not obey my teachers and I did not heed my instructors.

¹⁴ I almost came to complete ruin in the midst of the whole congregation!"

-PROVERBS 5:11-14 (NET)

Lesson:

Words of wisdom are usually only considered wise after one has failed. It doesn't have to be that way for children of God. This definition of unapologetic sets the tone for these lessons. *Unapologetic* is defined as *not acknowledging or expressing regret.* The above passage creates a scenario of what one might say at the end of their lives when they have lived in regret.

Regret Results:

1. They have groaned at the end of their lives.

2. Their flesh has wasted away.

3. Their body has wasted away.

4. They have regret because they hated discipline.

5. Their hearts rejected correction or reproof.

6. They admit they were disobedient.

7. They admit they did not listen to correction or reproof.

8. As a result of the above, they almost came to complete ruin.

All of this is laced with *regret*. The question that begs to be asked is, "Why should one live in regret when they can live unapologetically?" "How can we live without regret?"

In other words, "How can we live unapologetically?"

Consider the Following:

Think about your current actions, thoughts and lifestyle. Do they lead to productivity or groaning? Each step is either forward movement to productivity or a step backward toward failure. Whether that first step begins with a change of mind or change of heart, it is movement. Groaning conveys a sense of despair or pain. Has your pathway been filled with pain? Despair? Evaluate, recognize and rectify.

1. Consider that you didn't care for your body as you should have. As you age, your body may fail to

cooperate with your latest endeavors. In 1 Corinthians 9:27 (KJV), the Word says, *But I keep under my body, and bring it into subjection: lest that by any means, when I have preached to others, I myself should be a castaway.* What could you do now to partner with your body and the Holy Spirit—to Whom your body belongs—to fix this area of your life? Recognizing it now can turn the tide to give you longevity.

2. Discipline is your friend. The simplest definition of discipline is the practice of training. Training your thoughts. Training your body. Training your thinking. Training your emotions. Training your spiritual life through devotion. The Apostle Paul said that he kept his body under control so that he wouldn't be caught in the trap that he preached about. Correction and discipline empower and enable us to live powerful, unbothered, unapologetic lives.

3. The instructors in your life are there to pour into you the seeds of greatness and tools necessary for your progression. To ignore and disregard their words is to open the door to a life of regret. Take advantage of the seasoned ones in your life *now*.

Prayer:

Father, today I confess that I have not always followed the path that leads me forward. Forgive me. Redirect me. Open my ears that I may hear your voice through the words of the instructors that you have placed in my life. Please, give me the grace to move forward into an unapologetic life of joy, peace and success. *Amen.*

Grace Notes

LESSON #2
"Unapologetic Praise"

Foundational Scriptures:
2 Samuel 6:12-22

Key Verses:

¹⁴ And David danced before the LORD with all [his] might; and David [was] girded with a linen ephod.

¹⁵ So David and all the house of Israel brought up the ark of the LORD with shouting, and with the sound of the trumpet.

²² And I will yet be more vile than thus, and will be base in mine own sight: and of the maidservants which thou hast spoken of, of them shall I be had in honour.

–2 SAMUEL 6:14-15; 22

Lesson:

While reading this passage, I was reminded that my praise should be without pause, hesitation or regret. David, the sweet psalmist of Israel, was so filled with joy and worship for the Lord at the return of the Ark of the Covenant that his spouse was embarrassed at the caliber of his praise. David, however, was unapologetic.

David's praise and exuberance for what the Lord had done was, as described by his spouse, Michal, shameless. How right she was! He had no shame in his praise before the Lord. David knew that the Lord had brought him from tending sheep, to slaying a giant, to gaining favor with King Saul and, ultimately, to being the anointed one to rule in place of King Saul, Michal's father. What a long way from the pastures tending his father's sheep. By learning the lessons while tending to sheep, David was prepared for a life to be lived unapologetically in praise.

Consider the Following:

We must choose to offer praise daily—even sacrificial praise—to our Lord. Regardless of the opinions of others, we should not hold back on our exuberant praise for the great God we serve. Our meditation of Him should be often. Our thoughts about Him will create an undeniable expectation. Our faith toward Him will catapult us into the greatness He prepared for us.

Prayer:

Father, there are times that my praise is based on external circumstances rather than on the foundation of your continual goodness and blessings in my life. Remind me daily that, even if the sun isn't shining, you still reign in my life. Remind me to rejoice in your consistent faithfulness daily with unapologetic praise. *Amen.*

Grace Notes

LESSON #2—*Grace Notes*

LESSON #3
"Unapologetic Prayer"

Foundational Scriptures:
1 Samuel 2:1-10 (NLT)

Key Verses:

⁵ *But unto Hannah he gave a worthy portion; for he loved Hannah: but the LORD had shut up her womb.*

¹⁵ *And Hannah answered and said, No, my lord, I [am] a woman of a sorrowful spirit: I have drunk neither wine nor strong drink, but have poured out my soul before the LORD.*

¹⁶ *Count not thine handmaid for a daughter of Belial: for out of the abundance of my complaint and grief have I spoken hitherto.*

–1 SAMUEL 1:5; 15-16

Lesson:

Ooh! The blessedness of motherhood! To carry life within you and nurture that life to physical and spiritual maturity with kingdom purpose. Children were equated to having joy and blessings in the Bible. Unfortunately, Hannah was barren and was reminded daily by about her condition by her enemy, Peninnah (her husband's second wife). However, Hannah was unapologetic in her prayer. The depth of her need for a child caused her to pour out her heart to the Lord. God heard her *and* answered her prayer. Hannah's song is the culmination of her prayers. "Pesky Peninnah" finally met "Hilariously Happy Hannah"! Your adversary may believe that his antics have depleted your joy. That is the furthest thing from the truth! Pour out your heart in prayer to the Lord, who hears you and promises to answer when you call.

Consider the Following:

Though Hannah's husband, Elkanah, loved her deeply, his love could not fill the emptiness inside her. She wanted more. Do you have an adversary who taunts you because of what appears to be an unproductive, unfulfilled part of life that's beyond your control to fix? Prayer is your weapon. Sincere, unfettered, unapologetic prayer will produce a Samuel (asked of God) in your life. Don't let the delay in your answer keep you from standing in faith. Delay has the potential to enter your DNA and replicate itself into your offspring. This process of delay can certainly hinder your expectation of what God designed for you to accomplish. Unapologetically pray with expectation.

Prayer:

Father, help my unbelief. I have accepted the words of the adversary as truth. I now know that they are false. I believe what your Word says to me, about me. Your Word is truth. Let my will become agreeable with your Word. Line up my thoughts. I submit them to your Word and your will. As I do this, you will make me strong. *Amen.*

Grace Notes

LESSON #3 – *Grace Notes*

LESSON #4
"Unapologetic Hope"

Foundational Scriptures:
Mark 5:25–34; Luke 8:43–48

Key Verses:

[20] And, behold, a woman, which was diseased with an issue of blood twelve years, came behind [him], and touched the hem of his garment:

[21] For she said within herself, If I may but touch his garment, I shall be whole.

[22] But Jesus turned him about, and when he saw her, he said, Daughter, be of good comfort; thy faith hath made thee whole. And the woman was made whole from that hour.

–MATTHEW 9:20-22

Lesson:

"Is there any hope for me? I have suffered twelve years with this issue. I am financially depleted and can't hug my grandbabies. I have heard about a healer. I believe that if I can get close enough to touch the hem of His robe, I will receive healing. I don't want Him to see me because I have been spurned before. I just need to be in His presence, then my life would change. Others may not want me near because of my condition. *My condition is beyond my control!* Nevertheless, my hope is in Jesus. He is my hope. He is my *only* hope."

Consider the Following:

Hope is more than just thinking and wishing for the power of God to manifest in your life. Hope is expecting *with anticipation* a move of God after you pray.

Use all of your spiritual possessions of hope and faith. Together, they will change the dynamics of your life unapologetically.

Prayer:

Father, I am comforted in knowing that you see me. You see my pain. You see my issues. You see the length of time that I have struggled. Today, I turn to you as my hope. Give me grace to believe and receive with expectation a manifestation of your power in my situation. *Amen.*

Grace Notes

LESSON #4 – *Grace Notes*

LESSON #5
"Unapologetic Love"

Foundational Scriptures:
Luke 7:36-50

Key Verses:

³⁷ And, behold, a woman in the city, which was a sinner, when she knew that [Jesus] sat at meat in the Pharisee's house, brought an alabaster box of ointment,

³⁸ And stood at his feet behind [him] weeping, and began to wash his feet with tears, and did wipe [them] with the hairs of her head, and kissed his feet, and anointed [them] with the ointment.

⁵⁰ And he said to the woman, Thy faith hath saved thee; go in peace.

–LUKE 7:37-38; 50

Lesson:

There is an old hymn entitled, Come to Jesus. This broken and bruised woman came to Jesus—despite His present company—to receive what only He could give: forgiveness of her many sins and healing for her soul. Without hesitation, Jesus forgave her, healed her and stood for her while the town gossipers couldn't see beyond her reputation. Jesus knew there was more to her than what she had done.

Consider the Following:

How can we demonstrate the love of Jesus more to those who are living in sin? She was labeled a sinner. Apparently, everyone knew her deeds; however, no one knew her pain or saw her heart. Jesus saw both. How do *you* see others? I pray that our eyes would be enlightened and affect our hearts so we can see others through unapologetic loving eyes and hearts, like Jesus.

Prayer:

Father, you saw her deepest need; I know that you see mine. Heal me and save me. Help me to pour out my best to you with thanksgiving for your unapologetic love. *Amen.*

Grace Notes

LESSON #5 – *Grace Notes*

LESSON #6
"Unapologetic Peace"

Foundational Scriptures:

2 Kings 4:8-37; Psalm 119:165; Philippians 4:7

Key Verses:

[20] *And when he had taken him, and brought him to his mother, he sat on her knees till noon, and [then] died. ...*

[23] *And he said, Wherefore wilt thou go to him to day? [it is] neither new moon, nor sabbath. And she said, [It shall be] well.*

[26] *Run now, I pray thee, to meet her, and say unto her, [Is it] well with thee? [is it] well with thy husband? [is it] well with the child? And she answered, [It is] well.*

—2 KINGS 4:20; 23; 26

Lesson:

The Hebrew word *shalom* means "health, prosperity and peace."

"Sister All Is Well" (hereinafter "Sister AIW") had asked nothing of Elisha, yet the man of God wanted to bless her for her kindness in preparing a little room for him and his servant, as he often traveled through her area. Maybe she asked for nothing to avoid the disappointment of not receiving. Her encounter with the man of God was clear, even when the prophet asked her, "What can I do for you?"

Elisha thought maybe he could speak to the king or the captain of the host on her behalf; however, Sister AIW wanted nothing. But Gehazi, Elisha's observant servant, told him that she had no child and that her husband was old. Ah ha! Oh, you can see it! A deficit in need of a miracle! Sister AIW did have a desire. Maybe she thought that the combination of her husband's age and the fear of hoping again would leave her devastated. She needed a supernatural intervention!

The miracle child was conceived and born, and he grew into manhood. What could have been better to her than to have the stigma of barrenness taken away? She could now rejoice as a mother. However, there came a day when that joy was tested.

Sister AIW's son became ill and died; however, she was undaunted by the situation. She had learned to be at peace, even in the valley of the shadow of death. If God could make her elderly husband's seed live again, He could make her son live again.

Consider the Following:

In this valley of the shadow of death, her confession was the same: "All is well, and all shall be well." Oh! That we would not be shaken by what we see, hear or feel, but would maintain the posture that "all is well" and "all shall be well." The peace we have been promised surpasses our ability to comprehend. Sister AIW possessed a stillness and peace that kept her until she received another miracle. Praise God for her son living and breathing *again*.

May your peace flow during each test, trial and difficulty *unapologetically*.

Prayer:

Father, even in the darkest seasons of dread and despair, remind us that we can have the promised peace abundantly that we may walk unapologetically until we see the fulfillment of your promises. *Amen.*

Grace Notes

LESSON #6 – *Grace Notes*

LESSON #7
"Unapologetic Worship"

Foundational Scriptures:

2 Kings 3:11-25

Key Verses:

¹¹ But Jehoshaphat said, [Is there] not here a prophet of the LORD, that we may enquire of the LORD by him? And one of the king of Israel's servants answered and said, Here [is] Elisha the son of Shaphat, which poured water on the hands of Elijah.

¹² And Jehoshaphat said, The word of the LORD is with him. So the king of Israel and Jehoshaphat and the king of Edom went down to him.

¹⁵ But now bring me a minstrel. And it came to pass, when the minstrel played, that the hand of the LORD came upon him.

–2 KINGS 3:11-12; 15

Lesson:

There are many voices in our world. Some voices speak good and godliness, while others speak evil or whatever will bring pleasure to the listener. Elisha wasn't such a speaker; he would only speak what he heard. He only regarded the presence of the other kings because of the presence of King Jehoshaphat. However, Elisha required a musician to create an atmosphere of worship for him to hear the Word of the Lord regarding their matter. Elisha's worship was unapologetic in that he was certain of "this is how this works" and no other way. If you want the Lord to speak, worship.

Consider the Following:

Elisha knew that speaking what he wanted (good or bad) meant nothing—he could not guarantee victory for anyone. The same is true for us. Whatever the prescription for worship that brings the presence of God, we must conform to it and not to what brings us pleasure. Worship creates an entry into the presence of God. In His presence, there is fullness of joy. If we find the secret place where God is, and find the place where He is speaking, He will comfort our hearts and we will have unapologetic worship.

Prayer:

Father, help us to be open to the conduits you have set up for us to enter your presence. Heal us from the fear of the opinions of others. Help us to steer clear of being tainted by the ungodly voices in our world. We only want your hand to come upon us and give us direction. So, help us to submit to fit the format for unapologetic worship. *Amen*.

Grace Notes

LESSON #7 — *Grace Notes*

LESSON #8
"Unapologetic Healing"

Foundational Scriptures:
Acts 3:2-10

Key Verses:

² And a certain man lame from his mother's womb was carried, whom they laid daily at the gate of the temple which is called Beautiful, to ask alms of them that entered into the temple;

⁵ And he gave heed unto them, expecting to receive something of them.

⁷ And he took him by the right hand, and lifted [him] up: and immediately his feet and ankle bones received strength.

⁸ And he leaping up stood, and walked, and entered with them into the temple, walking, and leaping, and praising God.

–ACTS 3:2; 5; 7-8

Lesson:

Have you ever been pleasantly surprised to receive something you didn't even expect? You were overjoyed to receive it, all the while rejoicing. This man was taken to the Beautiful Gate daily to beg. However, I would think that he found no beauty in his plight, but it was all he had. One day, as he asked Peter and John for alms, these men did not respond as others had. They explained that they didn't have any money, but they had something that would change his life forever. They spoke with authority (Acts 3:6) and those words were *alive*! They touched his hand and, immediately, the lame man felt something in his lower extremities that he had not felt before. He was unapologetically *healed*, and his praise paralleled the power he felt in his body (Acts 3:8-9).

Consider the Following:

What is your response to an unexpected supernatural intervention? Our behavior and posture should not be dampened because others are not rejoicing with us. That deserves your best praise as healing is unapologetically yours!

Prayer:

Father, your Word is yet alive. Thank you that your Word is restructuring and renewing my strength so that I am unapologetically healed in every sphere of my body, soul and mind. Thank you. *Amen.*

Grace Notes

LESSON #8 – *Grace Notes*

LESSON #9
"Unapologetic Testimony"

Foundational Scriptures:
John 4:4-30; 39-42

Key Verses:

⁴ And he must needs go through Samaria.

²⁸ The woman then left her waterpot, and went her way into the city, and saith to the men,

²⁹ Come, see a man, which told me all things that ever I did: is not this the Christ?

³⁹ And many of the Samaritans of that city believed on him for the saying of the woman, which testified, He told me all that ever I did.

-JOHN 4:4; 28-29; 39

Lesson:

Testimonies are given by those who have witnessed an event or have information that will prove the facts of a matter. When the woman at the well met Jesus, she dialogued long enough to know that there was something different about Him. She was hungry for change as she told Him to give her the water that He offered. That is when her life changed. As a result, she could testify to others about the change that occurred.

Consider the Following:

According to the Scripture, Jesus needed to go through Samaria. He grew weary at a particular spot where He encountered a woman whose life needed change. Her testimony would be the catalyst for revival. Have we missed any divine encounters with those who need a change? Just like this woman's testimony brought revival to the entire city, one testimony of a changed life will be the catalyst for a move of God. How about you? Where is your unapologetic testimony that will ignite a fire in someone else?

Prayer:

Father, give us opportunities to share what you have done in our lives so the lives of others will be changed. Use me for your glory! *Amen.*

Grace Notes

LESSON #9 – *Grace Notes*

LESSON #10
"Unapologetic Change"

Foundational Scriptures:
John 4:4-30; 39-42

Key Verses:

15 The woman saith unto him, Sir, give me this water, that I thirst not, neither come hither to draw.

16 Jesus saith unto her, Go, call thy husband, and come hither.

17 The woman answered and said, I have no husband.

18 Jesus said unto her, Thou hast well said, I have no husband: For thou hast had five husbands; and he whom thou now hast is not thy husband: in that saidst thou truly.

–JOHN 4:15-18

Lesson:

Let's continue to look at the woman with the testimony. It is a testimony because everyone knew her. She said,

"Come see a man who has told me everything that I have done." Apparently, everyone else knew what she had done. She ran throughout the city, saying in essence, *"I am changed."* Come see the man who brought about this change. She may have thought it was a chance encounter, but Jesus was intentional in waiting for her to come to the well at an odd hour to fill her cup, change her life and satisfy the longing inside her.

Consider the Following:

Jesus is still changing lives today. The Scriptures said that He won't cast out those who come to Him. She wanted to be changed but was unaware of how to implement this change. Maybe she wanted a change in her relationship with men; however, this change eluded her. I believe Jesus needed to go through Samaria to have this encounter with this dear sister, whose unapologetic testimony of change would spark revival. Jesus remained there for two days, healing, teaching and changing lives.

Prayer:

Father, my prayer is simply that you would use me for your glory. Let the change in me be a manifestation of your power to those around me. Get the glory from my life. *Amen.*

Grace Notes

LESSON #10 – *Grace Notes*

LESSON #11
"Unapologetic Thanksgiving"

Foundational Scriptures:

Luke 1:39-55

Key Verses:

42 And she spake out with a loud voice, and said, Blessed [art] thou among women, and blessed [is] the fruit of thy womb.

45 And blessed [is] she that believed: for there shall be a performance of those things which were told her from the Lord.

46 And Mary said, My soul doth magnify the Lord,

47 And my spirit hath rejoiced in God my Saviour.

49 For he that is mighty hath done to me great things; and holy [is] his name.

—LUKE 1:42; 45-47; 49

Lesson:

When I think of the goodness and blessings from the Lover of my soul, my cup of joy and praise runs over! Thanksgiving is a natural byproduct when I contemplate what the Lord has done.

Consider the Following:

Contrast the awesomeness, wonder and amazement at the extremes of the two women in this passage. One receives a long-awaited son, who would be the forerunner of Jesus. The other receives the honor of birthing her Redeemer and the Savior of the world. Both gave God unapologetic thanksgiving for what He'd done. Shall we be mindful to have this same posture? Even when what the Lord is doing is not clear to us, we can certainly trust that He is faithful. God is faithful!

Prayer:

Father, give me your fresh perspective so that my thanksgiving is unashamedly unapologetic for all you've done and are doing for me. *Amen.*

Grace Notes

LESSON #11 – *Grace Notes*

LESSON #12
"Unapologetic Provision"

Foundational Scriptures:

1 Kings 17:1-16

Key Verses:

4 And it shall be, [that] thou shalt drink of the brook; and I have commanded the ravens to feed thee there.

7 And it came to pass after a while, that the brook dried up, because there had been no rain in the land.

9 Arise, get thee to Zarephath, which [belongeth] to Zidon, and dwell there: behold, I have commanded a widow woman there to sustain thee.

13 And Elijah said unto her, Fear not; go [and] do as thou hast said: but make me thereof a little cake first, and bring [it] unto me, and after make for thee and for thy son.

–1 KINGS 17:4; 7; 9; 13

Lesson:

The prophet, the ravens, and a widow depicted in this passage provide sufficient evidence of the Lord's ability to provide for us. Though Elijah spoke the word that created the drought, which impacted himself and the widow, the Lord was their provision. The prophet received instructions from the Lord about the safe location, where to receive sustenance, and who would feed him. When the brook dried up, as it does in the process of time, the Lord gave further directions to the prophet. Both the prophet and the widow needed miraculous provision and God had a plan.

Consider the Following:

Elijah's obedience was the key to their needs being met. The same is true for us. Our obedience to the voice of the Lord is essential to receiving our provisions. It is amazing how the passage says that the Lord commanded a widow to sustain the prophet; however, the widow wasn't informed about this agreement. There was something that the widow woman had and that was the heart to submit to the voice of the Lord. Her submission opened the door for miraculous, unapologetic provision for her, her son and the prophet.

Prayer:

Father, I believe that you are the same God who used the ravens and the widow to provide for the prophet. I believe that you will be my unapologetic provision in my times of need. *Amen.*

Grace Notes

LESSON #12 – *Grace Notes*

LESSON #13
"Unapologetic Favor"

Foundational Scriptures:
Genesis 12:1-3; 14:17-20; Deuteronomy 28:2-8

Key Verses:

Now the LORD had said unto Abram, Get thee out of thy country, and from thy kindred, and from thy father's house, unto a land that I will shew thee: And I will make of thee a great nation, and I will bless thee, and make thy name great; and thou shalt be a blessing: And I will bless them that bless thee, and curse him that curseth thee: and in thee shall all families of the earth be blessed.
—GENESIS 12:1-3

And he blessed him, and said, Blessed [be] Abram of the most high God, possessor of heaven and earth.
—GENESIS 14:19

All these blessings shall come on thee, and overtake thee, if thou shalt hearken unto the voice of the LORD thy God.
—DEUTERONOMY 28:2

Lesson:

Everyone loves to receive favor and blessings. Abram received a promise of multiplied favor, blessings and increase in his life. The promisor was God Jehovah, who never misleads or misrepresents His Word. The pronouncement of favor was followed by the manifestation of the blessings. Favor appeared to follow Abram wherever he went. God continually blessed him in every arena.

Consider the Following:

The promised blessings were initiated when Abram was asked to leave what was familiar to him, to no longer be content where he was and to trust God to fulfill every promise. What did Abram do? He obeyed God, and the blessings chased him down and overtook him. As we are faithfully obedient to God, we will find unapologetic favor in our lives.

Prayer:

Dear Father, as I read Your Word and believe that it is true for me, remind me continually never to be content with less than your best for me. Help me trust you, even if you call me out of my comfort zone into the unknown. You are faithful to fulfill every word you have spoken. *Amen.*

Grace Notes

LESSON #13 – *Grace Notes*

LESSON #14
"Unapologetic Protection and Blessings"

Foundational Scriptures:
Numbers 22; 23; 24

Key Verses:

⁶ Come now therefore, I pray thee, curse me this people; for they [are] too mighty for me: peradventure I shall prevail, [that] we may smite them, and [that] I may drive them out of the land: for I wot that he whom thou blessest [is] blessed, and he whom thou cursest is cursed.

¹⁸ And Balaam answered and said unto the servants of Balak, If Balak would give me his house full of silver and gold, I cannot go beyond the word of the LORD my God, to do less or more.

³⁸ And Balaam said unto Balak, Lo, I am come unto thee: have I now any power at all to say any thing? the word that God putteth in my mouth, that shall I speak.

-NUMBERS 22:6; 18; 38

> *⁸ How shall I curse, whom God hath not cursed?
> or how shall I defy, [whom] the LORD hath not defied?*
>
> *¹¹ And Balak said unto Balaam, What hast thou done unto me? I took thee to curse mine enemies, and, behold, thou hast blessed [them] altogether.*
>
> *¹² And he answered and said, Must I not take heed to speak that which the LORD hath put in my mouth?*
> —NUMBERS 23: 8; 11-12

Lesson:

The story of Balaam is filled with so many life lessons and nuances that are relevant to our lives. Balaam's reputation was that it would come to pass, if he said it. King Balak wanted that kind of prophet to curse Israel because his reputation preceded him. King Balak was afraid of losing his kingdom. Balaam refused to curse whom God had blessed and protected. In fact, Balaam couldn't curse Israel, no matter what he said or did. He had "met his match," so to speak, in that God protected Israel and blessed them wherever they went as long as they remained obedient to Him.

King Balak offered Balaam money, fame and all sorts of wonderful things to just pronounce a curse over Israel. Apparently, Balaam feared God more than he feared King Balak and more than he desired notoriety. We would do good to be reminded to follow suit. Whatever God's hand is on—fearful or not—we would do well to seek Him and follow His direction.

Consider the Following:

King Balak was willing to give anything for Israel to be cursed. He erroneously believed that if Balaam said it, it would be so. He was unfamiliar with the God of Israel who was greater than all he had ever heard about Balaam. Every time King Balak required Balaam to curse Israel, he pronounced a blessing. Balaam understood that he would be safest in obeying God, or the results would be catastrophic for him.

The odd thing is that Israel had no idea that all of this was going on behind the scenes. God was protecting and blessing them while they went along their way, "resting in the places He directed." Shouldn't that be our posture as we unapologetically possess the blessings and protection provided by our Father?

Prayer:

Father, amid the chaos in life, I am reminded that you are always looking out for me, my family and possessions. You have the best plans for my life. I don't need to be afraid because you are using someone to speak blessings and protection over me. Thank you that I will not live in regret for trusting your voice in situations beyond my control. I will say only what you say and believe you will perform your Word in my life. *Amen.*

Grace Notes

LESSON #14 – *Grace Notes*

LESSON #15
"Unapologetic Protection, Blessings and Favor"

Foundational Scriptures:
Numbers 22; 23; 24

Key Verses:

[19] God [is] not a man, that he should lie; neither the son of man, that he should repent: hath he said, and shall he not do [it]? or hath he spoken, and shall he not make it good?

[20] Behold, I have received [commandment] to bless: and he hath blessed; and I cannot reverse it.

[23] Surely [there is] no enchantment against Jacob, neither [is there] any divination against Israel: according to this time it shall be said of Jacob and of Israel, What hath God wrought!

[25] And Balak said unto Balaam, Neither curse them at all, nor bless them at all.

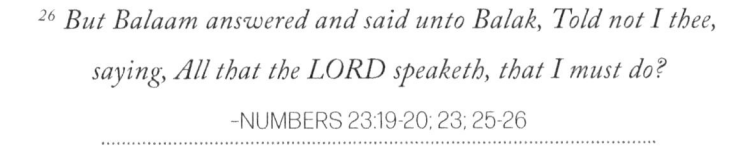

²⁶ But Balaam answered and said unto Balak, Told not I thee, saying, All that the LORD speaketh, that I must do?

-NUMBERS 23:19-20; 23; 25-26

¹⁰ And Balak's anger was kindled against Balaam, and he smote his hands together: and Balak said unto Balaam, I called thee to curse mine enemies, and, behold, thou hast altogether blessed [them] these three times.

¹¹ Therefore now flee thou to thy place: I thought to promote thee unto great honour; but, lo, the LORD hath kept thee back from honour.

¹³ If Balak would give me his house full of silver and gold, I cannot go beyond the commandment of the LORD, to do [either] good or bad of mine own mind; [but] what the LORD saith, that will I speak?

- NUMBERS 24:10-11; 13

Lesson:

As we peer further into the ministry of Balaam, we see that his relationship with the Lord God continued to grow. Though he was summoned to curse Israel, his concept of the power of God grew so much that he knew that if God blessed something, merely speaking words against it would not prove productive. No matter how often he was called upon to speak against Israel, he literally could not find the words. He could only bless whom God was blessing. Hallelujah!

Consider the Following:

Beloved, rest assured that no matter what plot or ploy the adversary forms against you, it can't work as long as you remain in the safe place of God's will and Word. As long as Israel remained faithful, devoted and loyal to God, blessings, protection and even favor were abundant in their lives. They truly lived unapologetically, covered by the favor of God. We, too, are recipients of this same protection, blessings and favor. Remind yourself continually that we have a better covenant and can live unapologetically in the protection, blessings and favor of God. No matter the adversary, we have the victory!

Prayer:

Thank you, Father, for this reminder that we are the unapologetic recipients of your protection, blessings and favor. *Amen.*

Grace Notes

LESSON #15 – *Grace Notes*

LESSON #16
"Unapologetic Power"

Foundational Scriptures:
Luke 17:12-14

Key Verses:

¹³ And they lifted up [their] voices, and said, Jesus, Master, have mercy on us. And when he saw [them], he said unto them, Go shew yourselves unto the priests.

¹⁴ And it came to pass, that, as they went, they were cleansed.
-LUKE 17:13-14

Lesson:

There is a song entitled, "Power Belongs to God". In this story of the ten lepers, Jesus demonstrated power—not by laying hands on the lepers who called out to Him for mercy—but by merely instructing them to do something that the law required. For lepers to be declared clean, the priest had to inspect their bodies to see if there was leprosy anywhere. Jesus told them to go, and they went. As they obeyed the command, the power of God was manifested, and their leprosy was gone!

Consider the Following:

The power that healed the ten lepers is still present today. It is at our disposal for healing. The Scriptures say that healing is the children's bread (Matthew 15:22-28). We are His children; therefore, we are candidates and recipients indeed of this unapologetic power. Obey and receive it *unapologetically*.

Prayer:

Father, we are so grateful that we can cry out for mercy as the lepers did and receive even greater from you as we are new covenant believers. Help us to obey your directions and receive the power available for us through the Word. *Amen*.

Grace Notes

LESSON #16 – *Grace Notes*

LESSON #17
"Unapologetic Witness"

Foundational Scriptures:
Luke 17:15-19

Key Verses:

15 And one of them, when he saw that he was healed, turned back, and with a loud voice glorified God,

19 And he said unto him, Arise, go thy way: thy faith hath made thee whole.

–LUKE 17:15; 19

Lesson:

Witnesses are those who possess evidence of an event that took place or an exchange of words. The witness gives their personal testimony of actual events. Jesus gave ten lepers instructions to show themselves to the priest so that they could be pronounced clean. However, as they were going, one of them saw what took place in his body by the power of the words spoken and he changed directions. He returned to give thanks. His life was changing, and he wanted to give praise and glory to God for this miracle. He wasn't waiting for the pronouncement of "clean" by the priest—he already knew he was clean. He had a testimony!

Consider the Following:

Only one of the previously unclean lepers returned to give glory to God. He did not want to remain with the others. He opted to turn back to say, "Thank you." Sometimes, we may be the only one who will give glory to God for what He has done and is doing in our lives. Jesus asked about the other nine lepers, but the healed man was not concerned about where they were at the moment. Beloved, never be afraid to be the one who will return to thank God for giving you an unapologetic testimony that demonstrates His love and power.

Prayer:

Father, I will be the one! I will remember to thank you for what you have done and are doing in my life. If no one else remembers, I will be the one with the unapologetic testimony! Thank you, Father. *Amen.*

Grace Notes

LESSON #17 – *Grace Notes*

LESSON #18
"Unapologetic Prosperity"

Foundational Scriptures:

2 Kings 4:1-2; 7

Key Verses:

¹ Now there cried a certain woman of the wives of the sons of the prophets unto Elisha, saying, Thy servant my husband is dead; and thou knowest that thy servant did fear the LORD: and the creditor is come to take unto him my two sons to be bondmen.

² And Elisha said unto her, What shall I do for thee? tell me, what hast thou in the house? And she said, Thine handmaid hath not any thing in the house, save a pot of oil.

⁷ Then she came and told the man of God. And he said, Go, sell the oil, and pay thy debt, and live thou and thy children of the rest.

–2 KINGS 4:1-2; 7

Lesson:

This widow had suffered much, and it wasn't over. Her husband died, leaving her in poverty with debt and children. She believed she had nothing that God could use to "fix" her situation. The prophet's words were, "What do you want me to do?" and "What do you have in your house?" There had to be a starting point. In other words, "There must be something in your house that God can use to create a miracle for you."

She didn't think that a pot of oil was significant. Naturally, it wasn't when compared to her enormous debt. However, it was enough for God to increase, multiply and use to change her financial landscape. God turned her situation around in the process of time and He still does today.

Consider the Following:

God gave Elisha wisdom to create a plan of action with clear instructions. The widow obeyed and, when she ran out of vessels, the oil stopped flowing. That one pot of oil created prosperity that could not be denied. God will prosper whatever you submit to Him. He is still in the business of giving His children ideas and inventions to bring unapologetic prosperity into their lives. Will you trust Him to change the landscape of every area of your life? As we yield to Him, He will do it.

Prayer:

Father, you are the God of more than enough. You promised to supply all of our needs according to your riches in glory. I believe that you will change the landscape of my life in every area that I speak to in faith. I am listening to your voice and obeying the principles in your Word. Thank you in advance for doors opened before me, for ways being made for me, and for unapologetic prosperity. *Amen.*

Grace Notes

LESSON #18 – *Grace Notes*

LESSON #19
"Unapologetically Repentant"

Foundational Scriptures:
2 Samuel 24; 1 Chronicles 21

Key Verses:

¹⁰ And David's heart smote him after that he had numbered the people. And David said unto the LORD, I have sinned greatly in that I have done: and now, I beseech thee, O LORD, take away the iniquity of thy servant; for I have done very foolishly.

²⁵ And David built there an altar unto the LORD, and offered burnt offerings and peace offerings. So the LORD was intreated for the land, and the plague was stayed from Israel.

–2 SAMUEL 24:10; 25

Lesson:

There are times when the snafus that we get ourselves into are our own making. This is the case with David in this passage. The enemy instigated it, and David fell prey to the tactic. David took a census of his kingdom, though he was clearly warned not to do so. This action caused judgment from God. David created it, and the people suffered.

When David realized what he had done, he had to choose one of three repercussions: three years of famine, three months to be destroyed by his enemies, or three days of pestilence in the land sent by the Lord. He chose the latter. Even that proved to be too much for him to bear. He repented and offered burnt offerings and peace offerings to the Lord. God heard him and stayed the destruction.

Consider the Following:

When God shuts a door, we can trust that whatever is behind that door isn't good for us. David messed up, invited the judgment of God into his nation, repented and then made a profound statement. He said that he would not offer God that which cost him nothing. Although we mess up, there is a price to be paid. It's not because God wants to punish us. We pay the price because we want God to see our repentant hearts. Whatever the price, I am willing to give it in order to keep the enemy at bay and the hand of God moving in my favor. May we all listen to the "stops" of God and follow with a soft, repentant heart unapologetically.

Prayer:

Father, keep our hearts soft and tender before you so that we will always trust you in our daily decisions. We desire that you be glorified in all we do and say. Help us to be quick to repent and turn from all that deprives us of your best *unapologetically*. Amen.

Grace Notes

LESSON #19 – *Grace Notes*

LESSON #20
"Unapologetic Love for Others"

Foundational Scriptures:
Luke 10:25-37

Key Verses:

²⁹ ...And who is my neighbour?

³⁰ And Jesus answering said, A certain [man] went down from Jerusalem to Jericho, and fell among thieves, which stripped him of his raiment, and wounded [him], and departed, leaving [him] half dead.

³⁶ Which now of these three, thinkest thou, was neighbour unto him that fell among the thieves?

³⁷ And he said, He that shewed mercy on him. Then said Jesus unto him, Go, and do thou likewise.

–LUKE 10:29-30; 36-37

Lesson:

Jesus is asked a question and answers with a parable. Jesus is asked to define the question, "Who is my neighbor?" He responds with a story of four men: one injured man, two religious men and one outcast. To give a clear definition, Jesus said that one man, a priest, passed by the injured man on the other side. Another man, a Levite, went for a closer look, but did nothing to help. The third man, a good Samaritan—an outcast and one who was not thought very well of by Jews—went over to the injured man, tended to his wounds by pouring in oil and wine, and took him to a place to receive care. The Samaritan left the injured man in the care of an innkeeper and promised to pay any additional expenses. In this passage, Jesus commands us to do likewise—to show mercy on others as the Samaritan demonstrated to the injured man.

Consider the Following:

Our neighbor is not limited to the family next door. Jesus' definition of a neighbor was someone who was unknown to any of the three men. What was key is that the neighbor was injured and needed someone to show him compassion and mercy. If we only see people as beneath us because of their condition, then our love will be limited. Love is powerful. Love will go the extra mile to make sure the neighbor's needs are met and that their healing begins. Having unapologetic love for others is a clear indicator of the love of Jesus that should abound in our hearts as children of God.

Prayer:

Father, help me to love my neighbor and show mercy as you consistently show your children. Help me to see the needs of others above my preferences. Help me to love others unapologetically as I demonstrate your love to them. *Amen.*

Grace Notes

LESSON #20 – *Grace Notes*

LESSON #21
"Unapologetic Sanctification"

Foundational Scriptures:
Isaiah 6:1-7

Key Verses:

¹ In the year that king Uzziah died I saw also the Lord sitting upon a throne, high and lifted up, and his train filled the temple.

⁵ Then said I, Woe [is] me! for I am undone; because I [am] a man of unclean lips, and I dwell in the midst of a people of unclean lips: for mine eyes have seen the King, the LORD of hosts.

⁷ And he laid [it] upon my mouth, and said, Lo, this hath touched thy lips; and thine iniquity is taken away, and thy sin purged.

—ISAIAH 6:1; 5; 7

Lesson:

Isaiah's encounter with the Lord changed his life. He saw his condition when he peered into the holiness of God. Some do not want to encounter the Lord because they love their darkness. The light of an encounter with the Lord clears the way for sanctification to begin and proceed in our lives. Isaiah's experience was earmarked by the death of King Uzziah.

Consider the Following:

Sometimes, there are things we will never encounter or be able to see until a thing dies. Sanctification is a kind of death of ourselves to ourselves—dying, but alive to the lordship of Christ. This death is not sad, but joyous, in that we can now live unapologetically sanctified in the presence of the Lord. Take the time today to reflect on how you might live a more sanctified life unto the Lord.

Prayer:

Father, give us an encounter with you that allows us to see what needs to die so that we can live unapologetically sanctified. *Amen.*

Grace Notes

LESSON #21 – *Grace Notes*

LESSON #22
"Unapologetic Miracles"

Foundational Scriptures:
Mark 5

Key Verses:

²⁴ And [Jesus] went with him; and much people followed him, and thronged him.

²⁷ When she had heard of Jesus, came in the press behind, and touched his garment.

²⁸ For she said, If I may touch but his clothes, I shall be whole.

²⁹ And straightway the fountain of her blood was dried up; and she felt in [her] body that she was healed of that plague.

³⁴ And he said unto her, Daughter, thy faith hath made thee whole; go in peace, and be whole of thy plague.

³⁵ While he yet spake, there came from the ruler of the synagogue's [house certain] which said, Thy daughter is dead: why troublest thou the Master any further?

³⁶ As soon as Jesus heard the word that was spoken, he saith unto the ruler of the synagogue, Be not afraid, only believe.

–MARK 5:24; 27-29; 34-36

Lesson:

This lesson could be titled "miracle in the middle of a miracle". Jesus was on His way to perform one miracle, while that miracle was interrupted by another miracle. Jesus was asked to heal Jairus' daughter and He agreed to go. However, on His way there, someone else called upon His anointing for their own miracle. She was not asking Jesus to call her name or speak over her. Her faith was sure. She believed that if she could touch His clothing, she'd be healed. What a novel approach! Her miracle depended less on Jesus and more on the direction of her faith in Him. She commanded a miraculous healing for her own life unapologetically while Jesus, the healer, was en route to heal someone else.

Consider the Following:

The supernatural intervention that you need is independent of someone to speak over you. However, it is definitely dependent on your faith in the healer. Faith comes by hearing and hearing comes by the Word of God. Do not be shy or reserved when what or who you need is close by. Reach out to Him and He will touch you, even if He is unaware at the moment. This woman wasn't intentionally delaying the healing of the child. Her interruption had more to do with her feelings of insignificance and her need to touch Him. Her faith was real as Jesus "felt" the power manifest, although He had not spoken or touched her. Wow! How powerful it is for us to touch Him and to receive without Him doing a thing!

Jesus said to this woman, "Your faith has made you whole." Though Jairus' daughter's miracle was delayed, and she actually died, Jesus reminded him to not fear, but only to believe. Apparently, he chose to believe in spite of what appeared to be the end and received a miracle for his daughter. Be healed, beloved, and receive your unapologetic miracle.

Prayer:

Dear Father, help us believe you, regardless of what we see, hear or feel. Empower us to stand on your Word despite appearances and the realities we see. We trust you to have the final say. Whatever you say is what we will agree with. Father, you watch over your Word to bring it to pass. Please bring it to pass in us. *Amen.*

Grace Notes

LESSON #22 – *Grace Notes*

LESSON #23
"Unapologetic Victory"

Foundational Scriptures:
Daniel 6:1-28

Key Verses:

10 Now when Daniel knew that the writing was signed, he went into his house; and his windows being open in his chamber toward Jerusalem, he kneeled upon his knees three times a day, and prayed, and gave thanks before his God, as he did aforetime.

11 Then these men assembled, and found Daniel praying and making supplication before his God.

—DANIEL 6:10-11

Lesson:

Daniel's story begins with favor from King Darius. He was a slave, but apparently, he stood out among the Hebrew slaves due to his skillset and abilities. This favor from the King led to jealousy rearing its ugly head in the leadership of the kingdom. So much so that an evil scheme was devised to kill Daniel and hopefully fill his position with a native citizen of the kingdom. The evil schemers implemented their plan with the King's signed decree, without their real motives being known. Daniel was unmoved by the royal decree that threatened his devotion to his God. Daniel continued to do as he had always done—he prayed.

Ultimately, Daniel was discovered disobeying the law by kneeling to pray to the Lord of heaven. He was sentenced to death and cast into the lion's den. God didn't protect Daniel before the test, trial and tribulation. He protected him in the middle of the situation. King Darius, though he loved Daniel, could not violate the law that he himself had signed. He realized that he was deceived. He had hoped that the God who Daniel served would deliver him.

The God of Daniel indeed stepped in and closed the mouths of the lions, causing Daniel to rest easy that night. The ultimate result was that God was glorified in the eyes of the King and the people, while Daniel's enemies were destroyed.

Consider the Following:

What a powerful demonstration and testimony of having conviction to encourage us today. Daniel, a committed servant of the Lord Jehovah, stood firm in the face of opposition by maintaining his devotional time. As you continue your walk with the Lord and your faith journey, remember that you, too, can have unapologetic victory. Victory only comes when one has endured without retreating. Building our foundation on the Word of God and our relationship with Him assures us that when our valley of the shadow of death arrives—as it certainly will—we will remain firm and resolute to assured victory *unapologetically*.

Prayer:

Father, I trust you to show up for me as I encounter difficulties in life. I believe that you are filling me with strength that will enable me to stand firm and resolute during seasons of testing. Help me to pass the test so that others will see and give you glory because of your faithfulness and favor. *Amen.*

Grace Notes

LESSON #23 – *Grace Notes*

LESSON #24
"Unapologetic Wisdom"

Foundational Scriptures:
Esther 3-8

Key Verses:

¹⁶ Go, gather together all the Jews that are present in Shushan, and fast ye for me, and neither eat nor drink three days, night or day: I also and my maidens will fast likewise; and so will I go in unto the king, which [is] not according to the law: and if I perish, I perish.

—ESTHER 4:16

Lesson:

Esther was an orphaned girl who became queen and ultimately saved the nation of Israel. A place was made for Esther before she ever knew it was being carved out for her. Queen Vashti was removed for her disrespect to King Ahasuerus, which created a vacancy to be filled by Esther. However, God's plan was bigger than a position for Esther.

God knew that wickedness was brewing for His children and created a plan to prevent their annihilation. What a mighty God we serve! If we only look out for ourselves, we miss God's plan for us. Mordecai was Esther's uncle, and he was pivotal in Esther's submission to the deliverance of Israel as she was strategically and divinely placed to be the mediator for Israel. She spoke the profound words that still ring today to encourage us.

"... I go in unto the king ... and if I perish, I perish."

Her wisdom in "how" to approach the king was paramount to getting her requests heard by him. Though Esther was the most beautiful woman in the land, and she was favored by the king, her wisdom opened doors for her that her exterior beauty alone could not.

Consider the Following:

As New Testament believers, we have promises from the Lord that if we are lacking in wisdom, we should ask Him. James 1:5-7 tells us that God gives wisdom liberally to *all* who ask. Wisdom isn't just about being smart or having information. Wisdom is knowing what to do with the information and when to do it. When we ask and receive from the Lord regarding life matters, we are completely unapologetic for the wisdom He promises and provides. We offer no apologies for the God-given wisdom that increases our productivity and increases in life. We choose to live unapologetically in wisdom.

Prayer:

Father, there are times when I don't know what to do or even the best approach to take regarding a matter. I am confident that you are keenly aware as you see and hear all. Give me wisdom so that I will know what to do, when to do it and how to do it. As our wisdom increases, let our understanding and peace be multiplied. *Amen.*

Grace Notes

LESSON #24 – *Grace Notes*

LESSON #25
"Unapologetic Confidence"

Foundational Scriptures:
Proverbs 31

Key Verses:

¹⁸ She perceiveth that her merchandise [is] good: her candle goeth not out by night.

-PROVERBS 31:18

Lesson:

In our world, there appears to be a thin line between arrogance and confidence. One is applauded, while the other is minimized. The world celebrates arrogance. Although it may be called other terms, arrogance is still the sister of pride. Confidence is having the security in oneself that, though the opinions of others may counter what we believe, we remain resolute in agreeing with the picture we have created. We don't deny the truth, but we don't agree with deceit either. For us to have success in any area of life, we must come to terms with what God has deposited in us is actually good. In this passage, *good* refers to being beneficial to others. Others can be in the marketplace or others can also be in our homes.

Consider the Following:

We must come to terms with speaking and believing that our Father has placed "good" in us. Alone, we are not good; however, with Him, goodness is in us, and it is following us. What we produce should reflect the "good" that is in us. The Lord has deposited in us His unique plan, purpose and pursuits. Our confidence can only be found securely in knowing, believing and even acting in a manner that aligns with this belief. God alone is our confidence. Once we accept this truth, we will recognize and receive that our merchandise is good, and we can live with unapologetic confidence.

Prayer:

Father, you provide such joy in our lives through your Scriptures. Today, we ask that you correct our thinking and belief system so that we will be confident in you and what you have deposited in us. We want to be examples to others that you have provided "good" for them, too. For all these things, we humbly give you thanks. *Amen*.

Grace Notes

LESSON #26
"Unapologetic Recovery"

Foundational Scriptures:
1 Samuel 30:1-18

Key Verses:

⁸ And David enquired at the LORD, saying, Shall I pursue after this troop? shall I overtake them? And he answered him, Pursue: for thou shalt surely overtake [them], and without fail recover [all].

–1 SAMUEL 30:8

Lesson:

Recover could be defined as to attain or to be able to secure, more than likely something that was lost, stolen or removed by someone other than the original owner. In this case, the families and the property of David and his men were taken by the Philistines. Some of them were so grief-stricken and despondent that they could not function enough to go with David. Actually, they were devastated and distraught by their loss that they thought of stoning David. You know how we do. Someone is to blame for this precarious predicament. David's posture was different.

David knew that the solution couldn't be found in blaming anyone or in crying. He knew that he had to hear from God. He understood that unless the Lord went before him and with him, he would need not go, as the end result would be failure. Upon asking God for direction, God responded with, "Go get your stuff and your families. You will recover everything." That's the translation that I hear! *Go get your stuff! I am going before you.* That was all of the assurance David needed. Others may not have the strength or power to pursue the enemy. But David? Oh, he knew that God going before them would allow them to unapologetically recover all.

Consider the Following:

How often do we relinquish victory because an adversary takes something from us? I am referring to being fearless in asking God for direction, then confidently going forward to possess (or repossess) your possessions. We must be unapologetic about our God providing the wherewithal to recover all that was stolen by the adversary for whatever reason. Let's pursue the greatness that God has for us so we will have unapologetic recovery.

Prayer:

Father, help us to seek you first in every situation. Remind us that you promised victory in our lives. We are utterly dependent on you to fight for us. When you are in it, we are certain that you will help us to recover all *unapologetically*. *Amen.*

Grace Notes

LESSON #28 – *Grace Notes*

LESSON #27
"Unapologetically Silencing the Enemy"

Foundational Scriptures:

Psalm 8:2; Matthew 21:16

Key Verses:

Out of the mouth of babes and sucklings hast thou ordained strength because of thine enemies, that thou mightest still the enemy and the avenger.

–PSALM 8:2

And said unto him, Hearest thou what these say? And Jesus saith unto them, Yea; have ye never read, Out of the mouth of babes and sucklings thou hast perfected praise?

–MATTHEW 21:16

Lesson:

Our greatest struggle many times can be the "noise" from opposing thoughts. This noise can manipulate us into believing the less-than-positive thoughts that loom largely in our minds. We must not consider this the norm for the believer. Those thoughts must be brought into captivity. The phrase, "that thou mightest still" clarifies when we see the meaning. It means, "to cease; to rest, desist from labour." This passage tells us that praise will cause the enemy to cease (his tactics); to rest (from taunting us) and to desist from labor (leaving us free from his plots, plans and ploys). We have been given the tools to silence the enemy, and they can be found in the strength received from praise.

Consider the Following:

Silencing the enemy begins with deciding that, when we give God our praise, it fills our atmosphere, thereby ordaining strength for the one praising God. Matthew 21:16 references a passage in Psalms. However, Matthew says that praise is "perfected." *Perfected* means "to mend what has been broken or torn." Praise God! It also means to "make one what he ought to be." Our praise is *strong*! No matter how big the adversary's voice is, we can unapologetically silence him with our praise to become what God intends for our lives.

Prayer:

Father, you have caused such a simple thing as praise to bring great strength to us just by opening our mouths and articulating words about who you are. This simple act also produces strength. There is enough strength in our praise that the adversary is silenced, and we are made whole. Thank you so much for giving us the power to silence the enemy with our praise *unapologetically. Amen.*

Grace Notes

LESSON #27 – *Grace Notes*

LESSON #28
"Unapologetically Inevitable"

Foundational Scriptures:

Isaiah 43:2 (NLT); Psalm 34:19; Psalm 34:19 (NLT); Romans 8:31 and Hebrews 13:5-6 (NLT)

Key Verses:

When you go through deep waters, I will be with you.
When you go through rivers of difficulty, you will not drown.
When you walk through the fire of oppression,
you will not be burned up; the flames will not consume you.
—ISAIAH 43:2 (NLT)

Many [are] the afflictions of the righteous: but the LORD delivereth him out of them all.
—PSALM 34:19

Lesson:

The word inevitable means that it is certain to happen; it is unavoidable and predictable. It's inevitable that we are going to experience some difficult and possibly challenging times in this life. It is what it is! But you know what else is inevitable (incapable of being avoided or prevented)? *God being with us always!* He promised never to leave us or forsake us. When times are good or bad, bad or good—it doesn't matter.

I smile when I consider the inevitability of God! Without regret or fear, I find great comfort in knowing that God is with us in every situation. It is *inevitable*! No matter how many difficulties, oppressions or fiery situations arise to destroy and consume my life, I stand unapologetically assured that God is with me inevitably.

Consider the Following:

God's promises are made good for His children. He will walk with us in the deep waters, rivers and fires. It is inevitable that these things will happen. However, it is also inevitable that He will be with us in each and every one of them. Praise our great God! As believers, we will face many troubles, but we can find great comfort in knowing that God will rescue us each time. God will snatch us away from the adversary and his plans.

Prayer:

Father, we are grateful that you are consistent in being with us. Remind us daily of your omnipresence in our lives. Never let us forget in the difficulties, or even in the pleasures, that we need you, and that you will be with us. We receive the truth that it is unapologetically inevitable that you will be a present help for us when we call. *Amen.*

Grace Notes

LESSON #28 – *Grace Notes*

LESSON #29
"Unapologetic Living"

Foundational Scriptures:
Philippians 1

Key Verses:
²¹ For to me to live [is] Christ, and to die [is] gain.
—PHILIPPIANS 1:21

Lesson:

In a time when everyone is concerned about protecting themselves from dying, this passage reminds us that there are obvious benefits to living an unapologetic life. Paul suggests that to remain in this body and exist is to benefit other believers. He was clear about his purpose for living. He was living to propagate the gospel. Although some were preaching about Jesus with impure motives, Paul was glad that Jesus was being preached. He was imprisoned at various times, but he understood that his situation did not hinder the preaching of the gospel. He knew that others were being bolder to preach because he was in prison. Paul was unapologetic about his plight: to live or to die. No matter the outcome, Paul wanted Christ to be glorified. Oh, that we, too, may we find this same disposition of unapologetic living!

Consider the Following:

If we all pour our lives into others, then our productivity/fruit will continue to produce forever. I believe this will create a situation where there is no fear in dying. We will have given all that we were destined to give and, therefore, can rejoice in a life well-lived. We have no power to control the lives of others, but we are responsible for pouring into them the truths that will enable them to grow and become all they are destined to be. For a well-lived believer, the fear of death is taken away when we are unapologetically living in this world while preparing for the world that is to come.

Prayer:

Father, help us to be sober in our thinking and expectations in this life. We want you to live through us so that we may die in you with no regrets. As we live in faith, help us to pour into others that same faith that they, too, may unapologetically live in this faith. *Amen.*

Grace Notes

LESSON #30
"Unapologetically His"

Foundational Scriptures:
Song of Solomon 2:16; Romans 14:8

Key Verses:

My beloved [is] mine, and I [am] his: he feedeth among the lilies.
—SONG OF SOLOMON 2:16

For whether we live, we live unto the Lord; and whether we die, we die unto the Lord: whether we live therefore, or die, we are the Lord's.
—ROMANS 14:8

Lesson:

I heard a song some decades ago that is filled with the words from Song of Solomon 2:16. The song ends with, "His banner over me is love." We all want to "belong" to someone. We want to bear their name, along with their children, if possible. The Lord of love promised to write our names on the palms of His hands (Isaiah 49:16), signifying the depth of His love for us. This should remind us of the significance that we have to Him. God loves us and always has our best interests at heart. As our relationship grows, so does my love for Him. He already loves us eternally. As difficult as that is to fathom with all of our flaws and issues, we are still unapologetically His!

Consider the Following:

There is no one who cares for us the way our Father does! His love is beyond words, and it provides comfort in all seasons of life. Paul said that we are the Lord's. We belong to Him whether in life or death. Knowing that we are His and He is ours, I can live a life unapologetically in peace that transcends all understanding. Today, I choose to live *unapologetically* His.

Prayer:

Father, thank you for wanting me and proving your love for me by sending Jesus to pay the price for my sins. You wanted a relationship so much for us that you provided all that was necessary and gave us free will to choose to love you back. I choose daily to love you back. I choose to hold nothing back from your loving eyes. Thank you for loving me and allowing me to be yours *unapologetically*. Amen.

Grace Notes

LESSON #30 – *Grace Notes*

About the Author

While many chase titles, fortune and fame, she's crystal clear that her purpose is only defined by God. As a minister, psalmist, speaker and author, Edna Jamison knows that she is not only called to share the Gospel in a unique, authentic way—but she is also called to usher believers into the life of abundance, peace and prosperity that God promised in His Word. On a mission to help others find their unique purpose and passion, Edna is the walking epitome of Ephesians 2:10, empowering others, "… to do good works, which God prepared in advance for us to do."

Ministering in some form or fashion since she was a child, Edna is no stranger to the ministerial marketplace. Serving as the founder and leader of *Graced for Today*, Edna strategically shares Biblical revelations via live videos on Facebook, YouTube, Instagram and Twitter. After many requests for an extended Bible study, Edna soon created L.I.F.E. (Live In Faith Everyday) Bible class where she teaches Biblical principles on Zoom and Facebook one Saturday a month. Listeners and viewers of all backgrounds leave inspired and motivated through the light of the Word—better positioning them to believe both that they are who God says they are and that He will do what He promised.

Holding a bachelor's degree in Liberal Arts, Edna is considering pursuing a master's degree in Marketing and preparing for a life-changing conference that will be spearheaded by *Graced for Today* titled "Illuminate". Continually expanding her product line, she also plans to launch a *Graced for Today* journal along with other products in the near future.

In her debut book, *30 Lessons on Unapologetic Living: Living Life Without Regret*, she uses modern-day parables and stories from the Word of God to give readers simple truths they can apply to everyday fruitful living. Short, but powerful, these lessons on life, leadership and God's perfect love challenges readers to live a life of victory and strength in spite of their external circumstances. For readers of all ages and faith levels, *30 Lessons on Unapologetic Living* can be indulged in as a daily devotional or a periodic jolt of hope.

For speaking engagements or booking, visit www.gracedfortoday.org, email edna.jamison@gracedfortoday.org or call 601.909.5580.

Made in United States
Orlando, FL
04 October 2022